HOW DO FLIES WALK UPSIDE DOWN?

Questions and Answers
About Insects

By Melvin and Gilda Berger
Illustrated by Jim Effler

SCHOLASTIC REFERENCE

Contents

KEY TO ABBREVIATIONS

cm = centimeter/centimetre
g = gram
kg = kilogram
km = kilometer/kilometre
km² = square kilometer/kilometre
mm = millimeter/millimetre
t = tonne

Library of Congress Cataloging-in-Publication Data

Berger, Melvin.
    How do flies walk upside down? / Melvin and Gilda Berger.
        p.   cm.
    Summary: A series of questions and answers provides information about the physical
    characteristics, senses, eating habits, life cycles, and behavior of different insects.
    1. Insects—Miscellanea—Juvenile literature. [1. Insects—Miscellanea. 2. Questions and
    answers.] I. Berger, Gilda. II. Title.
    Ql467.2.B475   1999   595.7—dc21   98-18457   CIP   AC

ISBN 0-590-13082-X (pob)
ISBN 0-439-08572-1 (pb)

Book design by David Saylor and Nancy Sabato

10 9 8 7 6 5 4 3 2 1   9/9 0/0 01 02 03

Printed in Mexico   49
First printing, August 1999

Expert reader: Louis Sorkin, B.C.E., Department of Entomology,
The American Museum of Natural History, New York, NY

The insect on the cover is a green bottle fly.

For Scott Chaskey of Quail Hill Farm

— M. AND G. BERGER

For my loving mother, Evelyn

— J. EFFLER

Introduction

Why read a question-and-answer book?

Because you're a kid! And kids are curious. It's natural—and important—to ask *questions* and look for *answers*. This book answers many questions that you may have:

- Do insects fall in love?
- Why do bees make honey?
- How do mosquitoes find you in the dark?
- Are all ladybugs ladies?
- Do all bees sting?
- How do fireflies make light?

Many of the answers will surprise and amaze you. We hope they'll tickle your imagination. Maybe they'll lead to *more questions* calling for *more answers*. That's what being curious is all about.

Melvin Berger

Gilda Berger

INSECT WAYS

How do flies walk upside down?

Easily! Flies have tiny claws at the ends of their feet that grip the rough spots on ceilings, windows, or walls. Also, their feet have hairy pads covered with a sticky substance that helps them cling to any surface. It's a little like walking with chewing gum on the bottom of your shoes.

Between the claws and the sticky stuff, flies can walk *anywhere* they want!

Are flies insects?

Yes. So are ants, bees, ladybugs, mosquitoes, butterflies, moths—and about one million other kinds of small animals. All adult insects have three parts to their body: head, thorax, and abdomen. The head has the eyes, mouth parts, and two antennae, or feelers. On the thorax most insects have six legs and either two or four wings. The abdomen is where the insect digests food and breathes.

Even with these three parts, most insects are less than $1/4$ inch (6.4 mm) long.

Are spiders insects?

No. Spiders belong to another group of small animals, called arachnids (uh-RAK-nidz). Other arachnids include ticks, mites, and scorpions.

Unlike insects, spiders have eight legs and only two parts to their body. Also, they have neither wings nor antennae. So *never* call a spider an insect!

Housefly

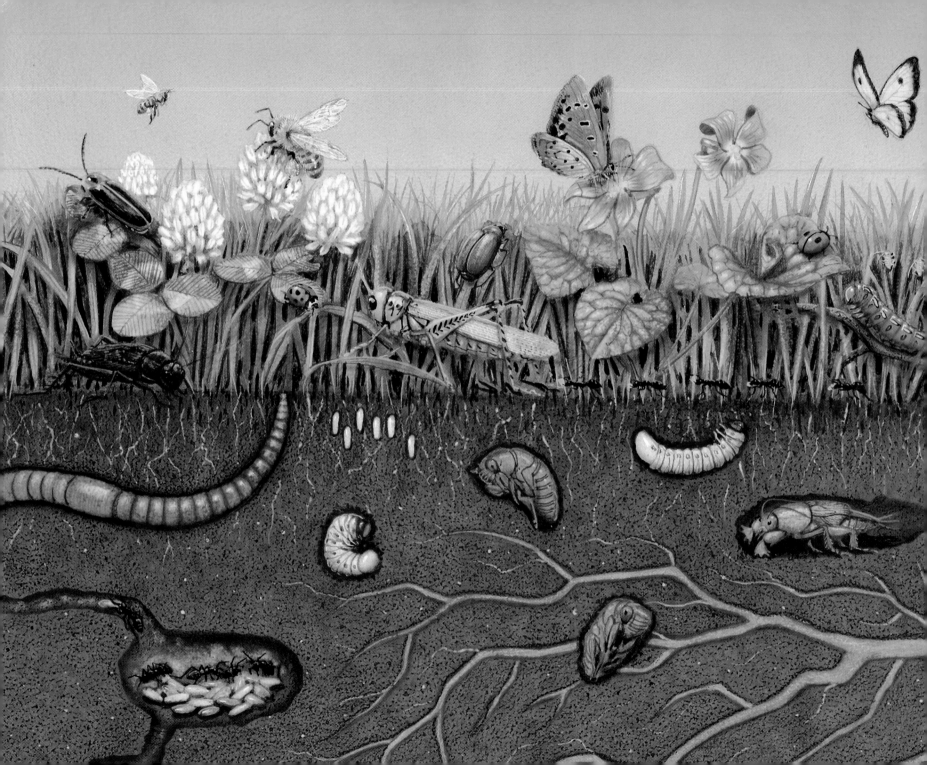

How many insects live in your backyard?

About 2,000 in every square yard (square meter) of soil.

Suppose you dug up 1 square mile (2.6 km²) of land. You'd find more than five and one-half billion insects. That is about the total number of people in the whole world! Scientists say insects outnumber people one million to one!

Who has been on Earth longer: insects or humans?

Insects, by far. The oldest insect fossils are at least 400 million years old. Compare that to the earliest humans. They appeared no more than four million years ago.

How many kinds of insects are there?

More than one million different species, or kinds. And scientists are still counting.

Every year, experts find up to 10,000 new species. They think there may be as many as 30 million species yet to be discovered. At this rate, it will take another 1,000 years to locate and identify all the insect species in the world!

Why are there so many insects?

A few reasons. Insects multiply very fast. Most females lay up to 200 eggs in a lifetime. A queen termite can lay more than 30,000 eggs a day!

Insects can survive the most difficult conditions on Earth. You can find insects at the North and South Poles and at the equator, in deserts and in jungles, under the ground and high in the air—and almost everywhere in between.

Insects are small. This means that each one needs little food and can easily hide from its enemies.

Do insects have bones?

No. Instead, every insect has an outside skeleton, called an exoskeleton. Attached to the exoskeleton are the insect's muscles. The exoskeleton protects the insect like a suit of armor.

As the insect grows bigger, its exoskeleton gets too tight. It splits open and the insect comes out. This is called molting. Then, a new and bigger exoskeleton hardens around the insect. Molting occurs again and again, until the insect is a full-sized adult.

Are insects strong?

Very. Some have as many as 4,000 separate muscles. That's a lot more than the 600 muscles in your body!

A bee, for example, can lift a load 300 times its own weight. If you were that strong, you could pick up a 10-ton (10.2 t) truck!

Cicada losing its exoskeleton

How do insects walk on six legs?

Easily. They move the front and back right legs at the same time as the middle left leg. Then they switch, moving the front and back left legs and middle right leg. This way they're always balanced on three legs.

Each of their six legs has five parts. Muscles attached to the thorax move the legs. Does it sound complicated? Be glad you have only two legs to worry about!

Do insects have blood?

Yes. But the blood is usually not red like your blood. Insect blood is generally light green, yellow, or colorless. And it doesn't flow through veins and arteries. The insect's heart pumps blood through all the empty spaces inside the insect's body.

Slap a mosquito and you may see red blood. But that's not the blood of the mosquito. It's your blood—or the blood the mosquito got from another person or from an animal.

How do insects breathe?

Through tiny holes along their sides. Insects have no lungs. Instead, the air passes from the holes into a large tube. This tube divides into small tubes. The small tubes divide into still smaller tubes. These very tiny tubes bring oxygen to every part of the body.

How do insects see?

With two large eyes that can take up most of an insect's head. Insect eyes are called compound eyes. Each compound eye is made up of many tiny lenses. A housefly's eye, for example, has 5,000 lenses. But dragonflies take the prize, with 30,000 lenses in each eye!

Insects can spot anything that is moving. Yet most don't see very well. The world looks blurry to them. And since insects don't have eyelids, their eyes are always open.

Do some insects have extra eyes?

Yes. Most adult insects also have three tiny simple eyes called ocelli (oh-SEL-eye). You can find them between the two compound eyes. The simple eyes cannot form images. They help the insect tell light from dark.

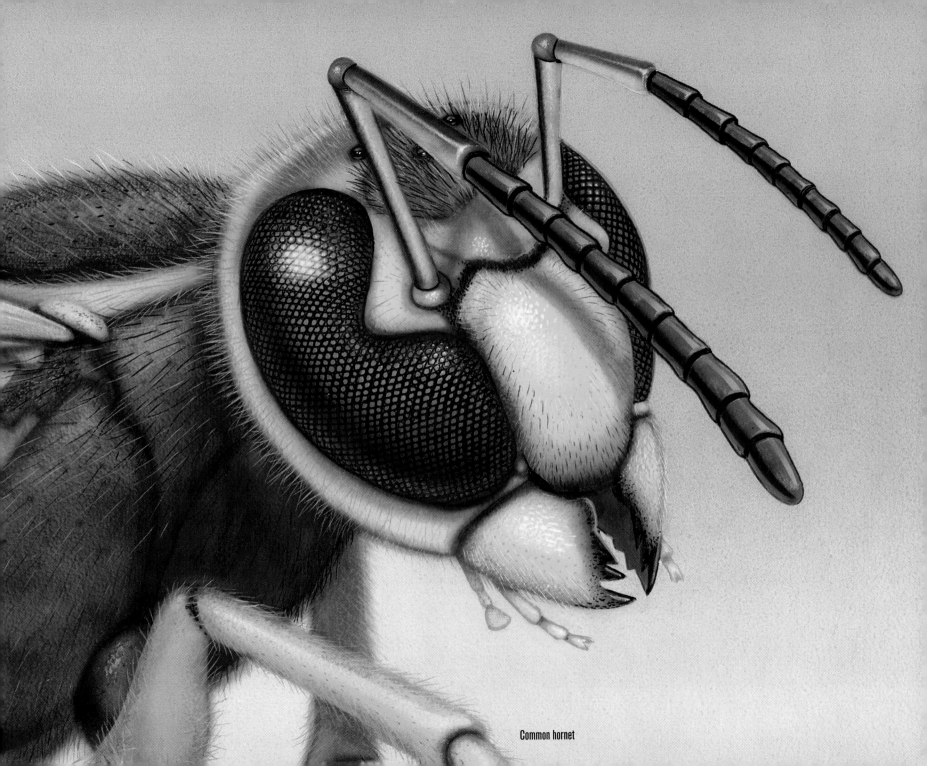

Common hornet

How do insects hear?

Not through ears like ours! Crickets hear through tiny openings on their front legs. Locusts, cicadas, and some kinds of moths and grasshoppers hear through little flat "ears" on their abdomens. Ants and mosquitoes hear with hairs on their antennae. Caterpillars receive sounds through hairs all over their bodies.

All sound is made by vibrations in the air. Insects pick up these vibrations and hear very well—even without ears like ours!

How do insects smell?

With antennae. The antennae of May beetles, for example, have 40,000 tiny pits. Each one is like a little nose for smelling. We wonder: If they catch cold, do they have 40,000 runny noses?

Many insects give off special chemicals that only other insects can sense. Antennae let each kind of insect find food, tell friend from foe, and spot danger. Some male moths can find female moths that are up to 7 miles (11.2 km) away—just by their smell!

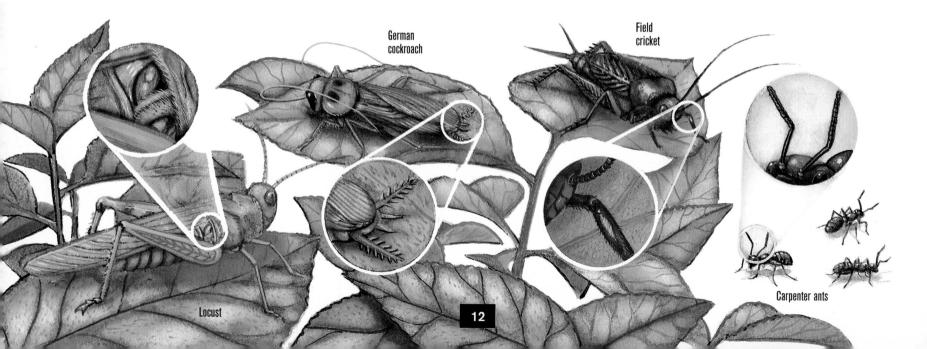

German cockroach

Field cricket

Carpenter ants

Locust

Do insects make sounds?

Yes. Many insects hum, buzz, or sing. But they don't make sounds the way you do. They have no vocal cords.

Whirring sounds come from rapidly flapping wings. Clicking and other sounds are made by rubbing body parts together—usually wing against wing or leg against wing. Male cicadas vibrate a thin skin on their abdomens. Their sounds can be heard for more than $1/4$ mile (0.4 km).

Sounds often help insects keep in touch with one another. But they're also used to warn of danger or to woo a mate.

True katydid

American bird
grasshopper

Gladiator katydid

Painted lady

American bumblebee

Eastern tailed blue

May beetle

Notch-tipped flower longhorn

Clouded sulfur

Do insects have a sense of touch?

Yes. Insects have a sense of touch that is far sharper than yours. Some of the short hairs that cover insects' antennae and bodies are connected to nerves and are very sensitive. They pick up the lightest pressure—even a little breeze.

The keen sense of touch helps most insects fly away before you can swat them. As soon as you move your hand, they feel the air moving. And away they go!

Do insects have tongues?

No. But insects have other ways to pick up various flavors.

Butterflies, moths, bees, and flies taste with their feet. Ants, wasps, and some bees taste through their antennae. Crickets and some wasps taste with the tips of their abdomens to find a good place for laying eggs.

What do insects eat?

Many different things. Butterflies, moths, flies, and mosquitoes are sucking insects. They feed on liquids. These insects use their mouth parts to suck up nectar and other fluids.

Grasshoppers, crickets, beetles, and termites are chewing insects. They eat plants and other solid foods. These insects use one pair of jaws to cut off bits of food and grind them down. Another pair of jaws helps to push the food down the throat.

A few insects, such as mayflies and some moths, never eat. That's because their lives are over in just a few hours or days. These insects become adults, lay eggs, and die.

Some insects are very heavy eaters. A silkworm eats enough leaves to increase its weight more than 4,000 times in just 56 days. A locust eats its own weight in plants every day. Just imagine eating *your* weight in food every day.

What eats insects?

Birds, frogs, lizards, skunks, anteaters, fish, and many other kinds of animals eat insects and insect eggs. Insects also eat other insects. Humans eat insects, too—like locusts, ants, caterpillars, and beetle larvae.

There are about 500 kinds of insect-eating plants. Perhaps you know the Venus flytrap best. It can catch an insect in the blink of an eye! Then it slowly digests the unlucky bug.

How do insects defend themselves?

Usually by escaping. They fly, run, or jump away. Many use camouflage. They blend in with their surroundings. Green caterpillars look like leaves. Gray and brown moths resemble the bark or moss on trees. When walking-stick insects sit on a branch, they look like twigs. The caterpillars that become giant swallowtail butterflies look like bird droppings.

Some insects fight back. Ladybugs, stick insects, cockroaches, and certain beetles give off bad-smelling liquids when enemies come too close. Some ants and beetles bite with their powerful jaws. Bees, wasps, and some ants sting.

Other insects have bright colors that warn away their enemies. Monarch butterflies taste bad, and birds have learned to leave them alone. Viceroy butterflies don't taste bad, but they look like monarchs and this keeps them safe.

Treehopper

True katydid

Bagworm
caterpillar

Variable
oakleaf
caterpillar

Brochymena

Giant
walkingstick

Large maple
pan worm

Green
stinkbug

Big poplar
sphinx

Giant swallowtail
caterpillar

Goliath beetle

Which is the biggest insect?

The Goliath beetle. At over 4 inches (10 cm) long, this insect is the size of a computer mouse! Also, it weighs nearly $1/4$ pound (100 g). This makes it the heaviest insect as well.

Another big insect is the Atlas moth. It has a wingspan of 12 inches (30 cm) from tip to tip.

About 1 foot (30 cm) in length, the tropical walkingstick is the longest insect on record. If you include its legs, the insect measures 20 inches (51 cm). This stick insect lives in the rain forests of Borneo.

Which is the smallest insect?

The fairyfly. It is only about $1/100$ of an inch (0.25 mm) long and is nearly invisible to the naked eye. In fact, the fairyfly is so tiny, it can fit through the eye of a small needle! Nearly 150 million of its eggs together weigh only 1 ounce (58 g).

How fast can insects fly?

Faster than you can run! Yellow jacket wasps can fly 15 miles (24 km) an hour. That's fast enough to catch you if you disturb a nest. Dragonflies are probably the fastest, at about 60 miles (96 km) an hour.

A no-see-um midge holds the record for wing speed. It flaps its wings nearly 63,000 times a minute!

Which insects run the fastest?

Cockroaches. They can reach speeds of $2^1/2$ miles (4 km) an hour. You may not think that is very fast. But at that speed they cover 40 body lengths a second. Compare this with human runners, who cover only four body lengths a second.

What happens to insects in the winter?

Many have laid eggs by then and died. In the spring, the eggs hatch and newborns emerge.

Others hide or hibernate in attics, cellars, barns, leaf piles, holes in trees, under bark, in caves, or in underground tunnels. While hibernating, the insects breathe more slowly and don't eat. When warm weather returns, they become active again.

Honeybees form big balls inside the hive. The bees on the inside shake and shiver to raise their body temperatures. The heat spreads out and warms all the bees.

Some insects migrate for the winter. Monarch butterflies fly south about 2,000 miles (3,200 km). At the beginning of spring, they head north.

Why don't hibernating insects freeze to death?

The blood of several kinds of insects contains a kind of antifreeze called glycerol (GLIHS-uh-rohl). This helps to keep them alive until warm weather returns.

The African midge can survive the very lowest temperatures. One was dipped in liquid helium at a temperature of −452 degrees Fahrenheit (−269°C), and it lived!

Can insects harm you?

Fewer than 10 percent of all insects bite or sting humans. Yet insects can—and do—cause enormous suffering. They can carry germs that cause yellow fever, cholera, typhus, and many other diseases. For example, every 10 seconds a person dies of malaria, a disease carried by certain mosquitoes. It is said that one-half of all human deaths throughout history were caused by mosquitoes.

Insects can be big pests. They eat about 10 percent of all food and fiber crops. They also harm cattle and sheep by spreading disease among them. Farmers spend about $7 billion a year to control pesky insects.

Monarch butterfly migration

GROWING UP

Do insects fall in love?

No. But insects do have ways of finding one another. Some female moths and male butterflies give off a special odor. Male grasshoppers, crickets, cicadas, and katydids sing. Both sexes of fireflies produce flashing lights. Female mosquitoes whirr their wings. And some male insects give their mates tasty bits of food to eat.

How are insects born?

Most hatch from tiny eggs laid by female insects. A few insects give birth to living young. These newborns hatch from eggs inside the female's body.

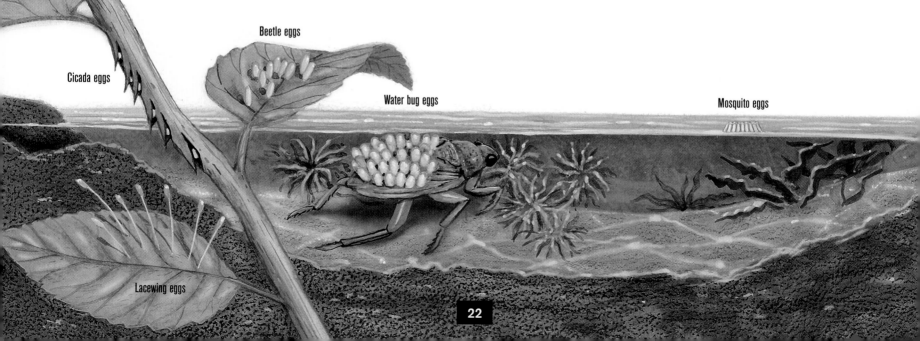

Beetle eggs

Cicada eggs

Water bug eggs

Mosquito eggs

Lacewing eggs

Where do insects lay their eggs?

In soil, on plants, in and on animal bodies, and in water. The place varies with the kind of insect. But each place supplies food to the insects that hatch from the eggs.

For example, the female horse botfly sticks her eggs to hairs on a horse's legs. The horse licks off the eggs. The eggs hatch and the young insects, called maggots, start to grow inside the horse's stomach!

Do insects ever sit on the eggs they lay?

No, but the adults of a few species do stay with the eggs. In certain of these species, adults protect and feed the young for some time after they hatch. But most female insects lay their eggs and then either leave or die.

Grasshopper
laying eggs

Cockroach
eggs

Ichneumon wasp

Do newborn insects look like their parents?

Not usually. Most newborn insects do not resemble the adults at all. In fact, they look so different that you can't tell they're the same species.

When they grow up, all insects of the same species will look alike. But first, almost every insect passes through a number of stages. The process is called metamorphosis.

What happens during metamorphosis?

Insects change. In butterflies, moths, beetles, flies, bees, wasps, ants, and most other insects, the change has four completely different stages: egg, larva (plural is larvae), pupa (plural is pupae), and adult. This is known as complete metamorphosis.

The four stages of complete metamorphosis

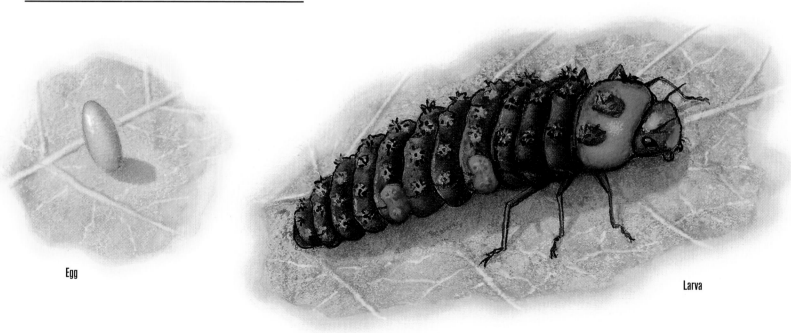

Egg

Larva

What do insect eggs look like?

Most are round in shape and light in color. But they can also be long or short, have ridges or be smooth. The eggs of very small insects are so tiny that they can be seen only under a microscope. But the eggs of big insects can be up to $1/2$ inch (13 mm) long. Insects lay their eggs either separately or in clumps.

What hatches from insect eggs in complete metamorphosis?

Wormlike or grublike larvae. Different species' larvae have different names. The larvae of moths and butterflies are called caterpillars. The larvae of some flies are called maggots. You might see them on dead animals or decayed meat. Some beetle larvae are known as grubs. Mosquito larvae are called wrigglers.

Pupa

Adult ladybug

What do larvae do?

Eat and eat and eat. One kind of moth larva eats 86,000 times its weight in the first two months of life. If you did the same, you'd put away 300 tons (305 t) of food!

Day by day, the larvae grow bigger. Since their outer skins can't expand, the insects molt. The young insects crawl out of the old skin. Then the new skin, which has been forming under the old skin, hardens. The insects may eat the skin they shed or leave it behind. It looks just like a real insect—except that it is hollow!

After larvae have molted several times, they finally stop eating and molt for the last time. Now when the skin splits, they are in an entirely new stage of life. They are pupae.

What are pupae?

A stage of development when insects are protected by a case, or covering. Most pupae look lifeless, but inside the case many big changes are taking place. The pupae are slowly turning into adult insects.

Larvae usually find well-hidden places in which to change into pupae. Beetle pupae can be buried deep in the soil. Most moth pupae are covered by cocoons. They might be hidden under a leaf or behind the bark of a tree. Butterfly pupae, called chrysalides (kruh-SAL-uh-deez), are usually attached to weeds or tree branches. Mud, stones, dead leaves, or rubbish protect some pupae.

How long does the pupal stage last?

Anywhere from a few days to over a year. The pupae are forming new body parts. Many kinds of insects spend the winter as pupae and emerge as adults in the spring. As adults, the insects are ready to mate and start the whole process all over again: egg, larva, pupa, and adult.

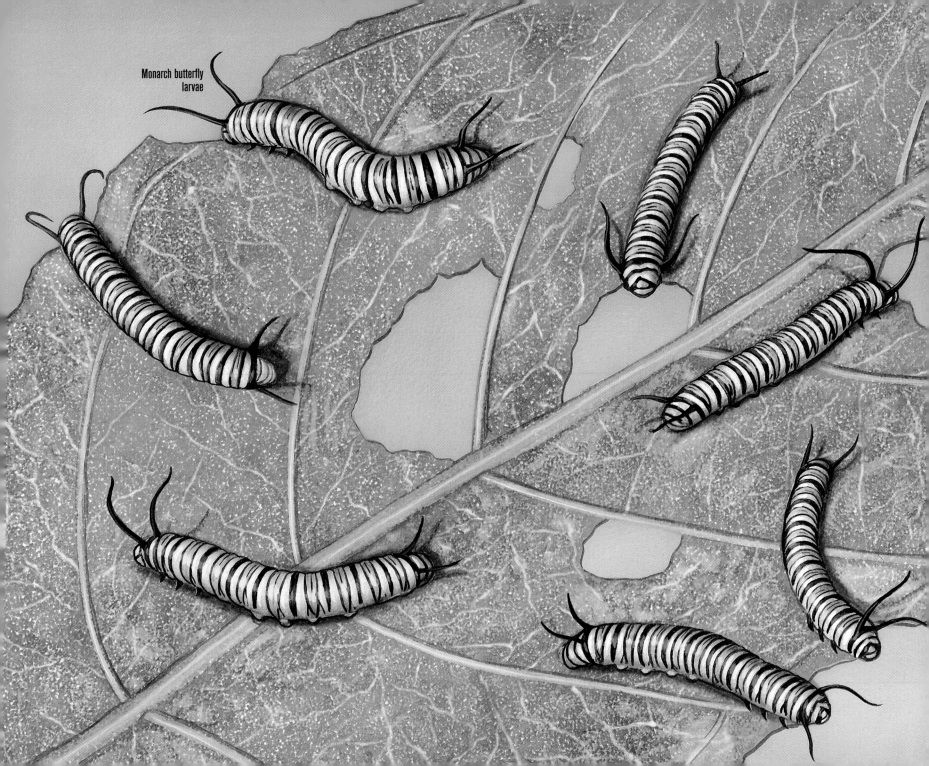

Monarch butterfly
larvae

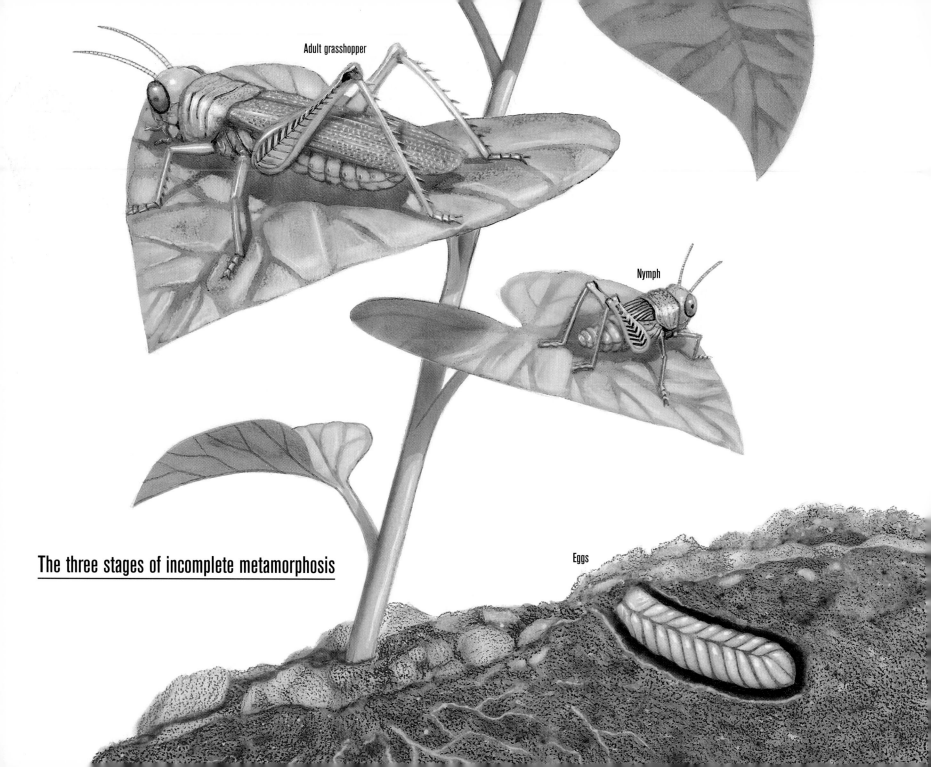

Adult grasshopper

Nymph

Eggs

The three stages of incomplete metamorphosis

Do all insects pass through four stages?

No. Grasshoppers, crickets, termites, mayflies, cockroaches, dragonflies, and some others go through only three stages: egg, nymph, and adult. This is known as incomplete metamorphosis.

The egg stage and adult stage are the same as in complete metamorphosis. Only the nymph stage is different.

Nymphs have unformed wings, are smaller than their parents, and are often not the same color. The nymphs gradually grow bigger and develop wings and reproductive organs.

When do nymphs grow wings?

The time varies. Grasshopper nymphs take about two months. During this time, the nymphs keep eating, growing, and molting. With each molt, they develop bigger and bigger wings. After about five molts, the nymphs are full grown. Now they have wings, just like their parents do.

Most dragonfly nymphs live in the water. Some take up to 5 years and 12 or more molts to become adults. They then crawl up out of the water, on plant stems. Soon they shed their final skin, open their wings, and fly away.

Do all insects go through metamorphosis?

No. A few, such as silverfish and springtails, simply grow bigger, much as you do. The newborns look just like their parents—except smaller. And from the time they hatch until they become adults, these animals hardly change their form or shape.

INSECTS YOU MIGHT MEET

Which insects live in your house?

The flies, mosquitoes, and ants you sometimes see, of course. But also many insects that keep out of sight.

The holes in your wool sweater were probably made by moth caterpillars or beetle larvae. Your dog scratches to get rid of tiny fleas. Hidden in your bookcase may be "bookworms," which are beetle larvae. And those fuzzy creatures you can find inside bad apples are the caterpillars of certain moths.

How can you tell a moth from a butterfly?

When at rest, a moth spreads its wings out flat to form a triangle. A butterfly holds its wings straight up, like sails on a boat.

Moths have feathery antennae without knobs. Butterfly antennae are slender, with knobs at the tips.

The bodies of most moths are thicker and furrier than those of butterflies. Moths fly mostly at night, while butterflies like sunlight and fly during the day.

What gives moth and butterfly wings their color?

Tiny, colorful, overlapping scales. Under a microscope they look like shingles on a roof. Some scales are colored red, orange, yellow, brown, black, or white. Others bend and scatter light, so they look blue, silver, violet, or green.

The colors may blend in with a background and help hide the butterfly. Or they may stand out and scare enemies away. Often the colors are meant to catch another butterfly's eye.

Giant swallowtail
butterfly

Promethea moth

How busy is a bee?

Very. A honeybee needs both nectar and pollen to live. To get these foods, the honeybee may visit 500 flowers in a single trip. The insect makes about 15 such trips on a sunny day, covering about $3\frac{1}{2}$ miles (5.6 km).

A bee must collect nectar from about 22 million flowers to make 1 pound (0.5 kg) of honey!

Why do honeybees make honey?

To feed the bees in their colony. A large colony of honeybees has up to 80,000 bees. They eat nearly 500 pounds (225 kg) of honey a year.

Honeybees collect nectar from flowers and bring it back to the hive, or nest. Other bees place the nectar into six-sided cells, where it changes into honey.

The bees eat some honey and feed some to the larvae. They store the rest for winter feeding or for rainy days. The stored honey is what beekeepers collect—and you eat.

Do all bees sting?

No. Only female bees can sting. Also, some kinds of bees have no stingers. Some have stingers but don't use them.

A honeybee has a barbed stinger at the back of its abdomen. Usually the bee keeps it hidden, but it's ready for use if needed.

A honeybee stings when in danger. It plunges the stinger into the victim's flesh. But as the bee flies away, the barbs hold fast. The stinger pulls out of the bee's body—and the bee soon dies.

Bee stings can be dangerous as well as painful. In the United States alone, about 40 people a year die from bee stings.

How do ants find your lunch in the park?

By smell. An ant finds a crumb you dropped. It carries the crumb back to the nest. As it goes, it presses its abdomen to the ground. This leaves a smell trail.

Back in the nest, the ant pokes the other ants. They run out and pick up the scent. By instinct, they follow the trail. Soon there are dozens of ants looking for more lunch crumbs.

Do ants have good eyesight?

Most ants can see nearby objects very well. But some are blind. To survive, all ants depend on a good sense of smell.

Ants smell with their antennae. Their antennae lead them to food and help them recognize friends and foes. Ants can live without seeing well. But if they lost their sense of smell, they'd die.

Are ants strong?

You bet. An ant can lift a weight 50 times as heavy as its body. If you were that strong, you could pick up a car weighing nearly 2 tons (2.1 t)!

Ants are also very fast walkers. The hotter it is, the faster they walk. Try shading some ants with a piece of cardboard on a hot, sunny day, and watch them slow down.

How did army ants get their name?

From the way they march along in huge troops of between 10,000 and 30,000,000 soldiers! Their feet make a loud rustling noise as they walk. Some people find this the scariest animal sound in the world.

Army ants also give off a smell like rotting meat. Often they kill and eat other insects, spiders, or larger animals that do not escape in time.

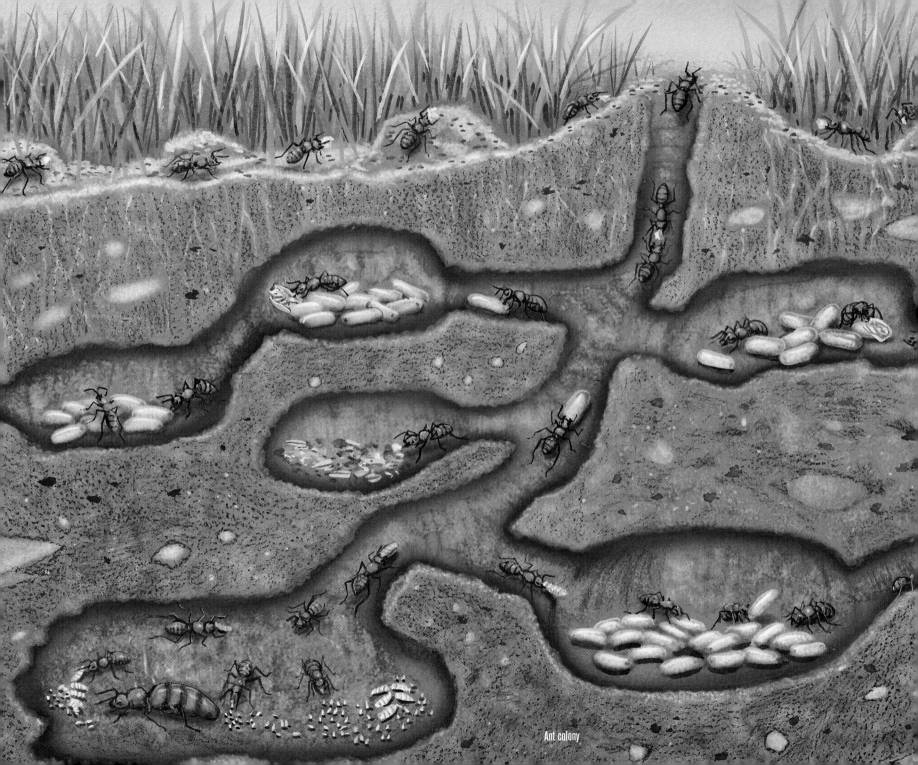

Ant colony

Do flies taste with their tongues?

No—mostly because they don't have tongues! Flies taste with their feet. First they step on food. If their feet tell them it tastes good, they eat it.

But flies can't eat solid foods. They can only sip liquids. House flies and fruit flies soak up liquids with their mouth parts and then sip the liquid. Or they drop saliva on solid food, changing it into a liquid that they then drink. Sand flies, stable flies, and female mosquitoes have sharp mouth parts. They stab the victim and then sip its blood.

Are flies dirty?

Not all of them. Flies that live in dirty surroundings are dirty. A fly may walk around on rotting food, garbage, and other filth. Germs stick to its legs, mouth parts, and hairy body. Its legs alone may have over one million germs!

If you see a fly near your sandwich, shoo it away. Flies that touch your food may leave harmful germs behind.

Which flies are like helicopters?

The hoverfly, bee fly, and flower fly. Most flies can only fly forward. But these three can fly forward *and* backward. They can even hover in place.

Which is the meanest fly?

A kind of gall midge fly. Gall midge flies are born inside their mother's body. Once born, they start eating her insides! In about two days they have eaten her whole body. The newborns then crawl out, leaving behind the hard, empty shell of the mother. Talk about rotten kids!

What was the biggest insect on Earth?

A dragonfly that lived about 310 million years ago. The insect had a wingspan of $27\frac{1}{2}$ inches (69.9 cm)! That's about the distance from the tip of your nose to the end of your arm. The biggest dragonfly today has a wingspan of less than 5 inches (12.7 cm).

Are dragonflies flies?

They're insects, but not flies. Dragonflies have two pairs of wings; flies have one pair. Dragonflies chew their food; flies can only drink liquids. Dragonflies pass through one (nymph) stage between egg and adult; flies pass through two separate stages, larva and pupa.

What do dragonflies eat?

Other insects. And do they eat! A dragonfly can eat its own weight in an hour. It takes you a couple of weeks to eat your weight in food. In one experiment, a scientist fed a dragonfly 40 large horseflies in two hours—and the dragonfly was still hungry!

How fast can dragonflies walk?

They can't walk at all! Like all insects, a dragonfly has six legs. But the legs do not work in the usual way. A dragonfly bends its legs to form a basket to hold other insects captured in flight. They often eat their prey in flight.

How do dragonflies hear?

They don't. As far as scientists can tell, dragonflies are deaf.

Dragonflies

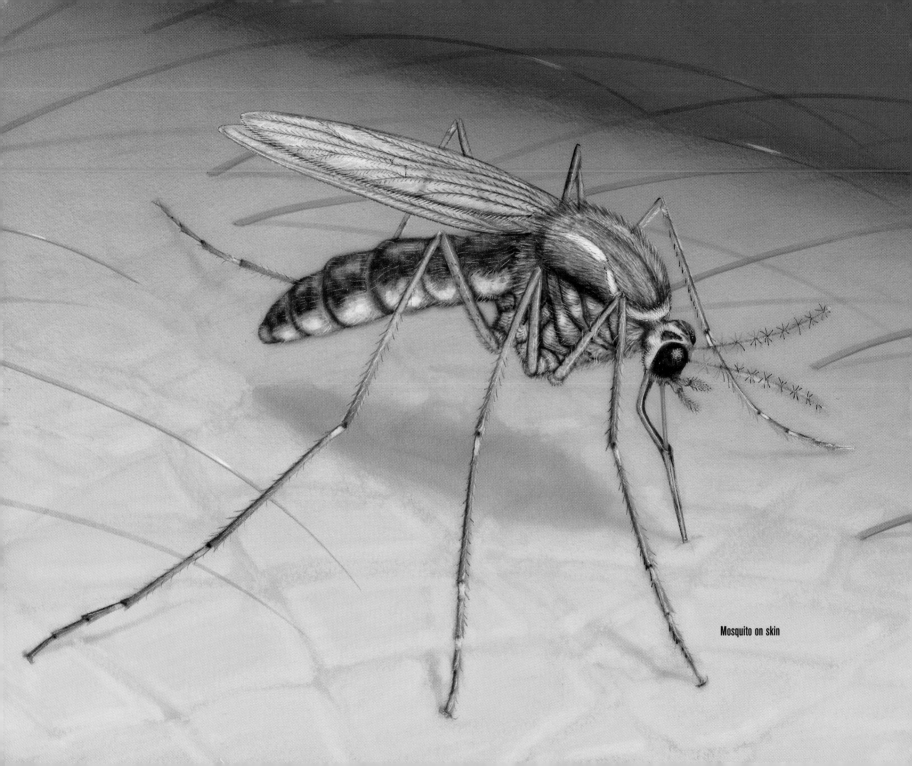
Mosquito on skin

Do mosquitoes bite?

Not really. Mosquitoes don't have jaws. But female mosquitoes do have sharp, pointed mouth parts that can stab the skin. With each stab, the mosquito also forces saliva into the wound. This stops the blood from clotting. Then she sucks up some blood, which she needs to make eggs. The amount of blood that mosquitoes take varies from species to species. But some may drink as much as one and one-quarter times their own weight at a time.

How do mosquitoes find you in the dark?

By your smell. Mosquitoes pick up the smell of your breath and body with their antennae. Then they swoop down, take a quick sip of blood, and fly away—sometimes before you feel anything!

Are mosquitoes dangerous?

Yes. Mosquitoes spread many serious diseases. The female of one species carries the germs that cause malaria, a disease that kills about one million people a year. Another species may infect people with yellow fever.

Mosquitoes once helped defeat the French general Napoléon. In 1803, Napoléon sent 25,000 troops to capture the island of Haiti. But 20,000 of his men died of yellow fever— and Napoléon headed home.

Where do mosquitoes live?

All over the world—from steamy tropics to ice-cold polar regions. Mosquitoes are more widely scattered than any other insect.

Which insects are built like armored tanks?

Beetles. Beetles have an exoskeleton, like other insects. But most also have a pair of hard front wings that cover their bodies. Beetles are the most common insects in the world. There are more beetles on Earth than any other living creature. Altogether, there are about 340,000 different kinds of beetles, including ladybugs and fireflies.

Are all ladybugs ladies?

No. Ladybugs are male *or* female. But none are very nice when attacked. They squirt a foul-smelling liquid from their knees. This disgusting spray is enough to turn away the bravest frog or bird.

Ladybugs are among our best friends. Their larvae eat other little insects, like aphids, that harm crops.

Do all ladybugs have spots?

No. Some have no spots. Others have between 2 and 15 spots. A ladybug's spots do not change with age, so counting spots won't tell you how old a ladybug is.

How do fireflies make their light?

With special chemicals inside their body. When the chemicals mix together—ZAP!—they light up.

Male fireflies flash their lights to find mates. As they fly through the air, each flashes his own special pattern of light signals.

Some female fireflies wait on the ground. At the right light signal, a female beams out her answer. The lights let the two fireflies find each other.

Twice-stabbed
ladybug

Nine-spotted ladybug

Fifteen-spotted
ladybug

Two-spotted
ladybug

Field crickets

Are crickets jumpers or flyers?

Mostly jumpers. Some crickets have wings and can fly. Yet we usually see them hopping from place to place.

Grasshoppers are jumpers, too. Some also have wings. But they seem to spring around more than they fly in the air.

How did the cricket get its name?

From the sound it makes—crick-et, crick-et, crick-et. It makes this cheerful noise by rubbing one rough wing over the other.

It's mostly the male crickets that chirp. Their songs seem to say, "Here I am. I'm looking for a mate." If the males stay in one spot, the females will soon find them.

Do crickets make good pets?

People in China think so. They keep crickets in cages and feed them cucumber and lettuce. It is a tradition to place food on tiny blue-and-white dishes. Each cage also has a water dish and a sleeping box. People who keep pet crickets usually keep them caged for a while and then set them free.

In Japan, people keep tree crickets as watchdogs. The crickets chirp all the time—except when a person or large animal comes near. If the crickets grow silent, people know someone is close.

Can crickets tell you the temperature?

Yes. The chirping of tree crickets speeds up as the temperature rises.

Tree cricket chirps are a common sound on summer days and nights. Count the number of chirps you hear in 15 seconds. Add 40 to the number. That will give you the temperature in degrees Fahrenheit. (For the approximate Celsius, subtract 32 from the Fahrenheit and divide by 2.)

Which insect has the strongest legs?

The grasshopper. A grasshopper can jump 500 times its own height. If your legs were that powerful, you could jump up nearly $\frac{1}{2}$ mile (0.8 km)! That's five times as high as the Washington Monument.

Did a grasshopper ever mistake a scientist for a grasshopper?

Yes! A scientist learned to imitate the sound of a female grasshopper. Once he made the sound while holding a male grasshopper in his hand. The grasshopper jumped up the scientist's arm and onto his shoulder. It was heading toward his mouth when the scientist ended the experiment!

When did a grasshopper start a war?

In 1872. Until then, the Delaware and Shawnee Indian tribes lived together in Pennsylvania. That year two boys, one from each tribe, argued over who owned a pet grasshopper. The argument grew and grew until the two tribes were at war!

What would the world be like without insects?

Grim. Without insects, there would be no fruits or vegetables. Insects carry the pollen that these plants need to grow.

Without insects, there would be far fewer kinds of birds, fish, and other animals. Many animals depend on insects for food.

Without insects, the earth would be littered with dead animals and plants. Insects eat the remains and help keep the earth clean.

Without insects, the world would be duller and quieter. There would be no brightly colored butterflies, no chirping crickets, and no flickering fireflies.

Some insects are pests. But most are friends. They help make our world what it is!

Firefly

Index

About the Authors

The Bergers grew up in New York City, where insects are few and far between. "Now that we live in the country," they say, "bees, ants, butterflies, ladybugs, fireflies, crickets, and many, MANY other small, six-legged animals are our closest neighbors."

About the Illustrator

Jim Effler has been drawing since he was two years old. That was 40 years ago! He enjoys looking for details in natural things. Jim lives in Cincinnati with his wife, Debbie, and his daughters, Jenna and Ariana.